THE RULE OF THREE

Ebb Tide

If ever known, I have forgotten now
My kinship with the moon;
Desire lures: I have forgotten how
The sirens bait their song,
Or why the little fishes rise
On lines of fate to kiss
Their bright reflections in the sky-glass.
What I was once is where the sea is.

Low tide, high noon; the cold-eyed
Spirits of thermals scale the sky
On suave spirals. Streams slide
Seaward down on twisting threads,
And all that has life, by escalade
Or abseil, traces the lines of its salt
Longing back to their source. Cradle
And tomb rock on the sea's bed.

Or so it seems; but I know a place
Where no-man builds his house:
Below the gull-haunted cliffs, below clefts
Where libidinous actinia droop like breasts,
Below all this stark, unbridled thirst
There is an emptiness where not to desire
Is a lack worse than wanting. Salt air
Swings like a door to nowhere.

I am the halfway house of the unpossessed,
I am one vast window, I am roofless;
I am vacancy meditating on stasis.
Time has cast and recast its nets
Through my mind, and it has found
Nothing but an hourglass in a sea of sand.
Once, when the slack tide stiffened to possess
Me, I rose to inherit the land.

THE RULE
OF
THREE

Elizabeth Garrett

BLOODAXE BOOKS

Copyright © Elizabeth Garrett 1991

ISBN: 1 85224 162 4

First published 1991 by
Bloodaxe Books Ltd,
P.O. Box 1SN,
Newcastle upon Tyne NE99 1SN.

Bloodaxe Books Ltd acknowledges
the financial assistance of Northern Arts.

Cover reproduction by V & H Reprographics, Newcastle upon Tyne.

Printed in Great Britain by
Bell & Bain Limited, Glasgow, Scotland.

For Philip

Acknowledgements

Acknowledgements are due to the editors of the following publications in which some of these poems first appeared: *First and Always: Poems for the Great Ormond Street Children's Hospital* (Faber, 1988), *Frogmore Papers, Frogmore Poetry: An Anthology* (Crabflower Pamphlets, 1989), *New Poetry from Oxford, The Orange Dove of Fiji: Poems for the Worldwide Fund for Nature* (Hutchinson, 1989), *Oxford Poetry, Poetry Review, Seven Years On: The Green Book Poets 1979-1986* (Green Book Press, 1986), *Slipping Glimpses: Poetry Book Society Supple-ment* (PBS/Hutchinson, 1985), *South West Review*, and *South West Review: A Celebration* (South West Arts, 1985).

Thirteen of these poems first appeared in Elizabeth Garrett's pamphlet *The Mortal Light* (Mandeville Press, 1990). The sequence 'Rumaucourt' appeared in Carol Rumens' anthology *New Women Poets* (Bloodaxe Books, 1990). 'History Goes to Work' was broadcast on *Poetry Now* (BBC Radio 3).

Contents

Envoi

These things, among the many
Gone, unnumbered and unmeasured
Into the slipstream of memory

I pick like random treasures
From a riverbed. Turning them
In my hand, I measure

Love's time — the current running
From heart to groin: our shadows
Coupled below us, although unseen

Even by us, in the shallows
Of the River Cover. Let them lie there
As long as love allows.

Russian Dolly

Down decades, centripetal, like a Russian dolly,
I unpack these bright impenetrable women.
Beside a pond, when the gift first came to me

Of knowing ignorance, where frogs grappled
In desperate scrum, I pared my curiosity
To taste beyond the hard gloss of an apple.

Dream fruit, the ever smaller seed within
The seed, down to this last generation's
Flowering of bright impenetrable women.

I took my wooden matron. And where the spikeless
Roses wreathed her apron-strings, I split
Her open. Inside, her smaller smiling likeness,

And inside her, and inside her again –
I understood the game, but could not see
The joke, nor how the game should end.

In broken calm, between the glaucous bloom
Of frogspawn, wooden faces wobble up
At me. Their upturned skirts, like currachs blown

From girdled shores, turn silently, and turn.
Around my waist the spikeless roses twine.

Two Floras
(after Botticelli and Titian)

What if these two should meet –
After hours, on naked feet,
Their artless déshabillé
Turning no heads, no Roman eyes –
In some corridor of the Uffizi?

The one, with the chest of a child,
Dancing from her millefiori
Grove, light as a spore
On the wind, spilling
Flowers on the polished floor;

The other, loosening her shift
Irrevocably so she slips from her frame,
One breast exposed, slow, in her soft
Mass of flesh, cupping
The incidental rose.

And what if they should? –
There would be little to say
With only the language of flowers:
But differences, in the shrewd, mute way
Of women, would be observed.

The one, troubled by the other's lack
Of scent, the absence of her shadow,
The flowers of make-believe
That blossom from her lap
Where no men go;

The other, meeting gravity for the first time,
Checked in her weightless dance,
Senses power in the flesh's substance,
Its smell – of more than flowers –
And the coloured shadow it casts.

La Maddalena
(after Piero della Francesca)

History has left her whole
As he painted her:
Intact, yet known,
The oblique moon her halo
In the vast twilight of the Duomo,
Pausing against the night.

How, then, did this man
Make this woman equivocate?
How fix with homely egg-yolk
Dignity (a glass casket
In her palm) with sensuality
(Bearing incense, as light)?

Still she comes, the loose shawl
Of her hair across her shoulders
Thrown. A particoloured cloak
Of wine and white, caught up
Across her thighs, casts upward
Pink along her neck and cheek.

What woman (if only in her dreams)
Has never held a light
Up to her breast, a cloth
Across her thighs in chasteness
And in welcome? This is
No anomaly, no artifice,

Nor merely man's conceit.
That purity, and knowledge
Of such loveliness, across a lucid
Brow, a shameless neck consort –
Is testament of woman: more whole
Than any virgin, bearing flesh as soul.

Fata Morgana

Guess who? – the sudden cool
Of fingers laid across your eyes.
A sort of nakedness that surprises
Like a breast disclosed, a full
Moon rising in the west – is this
Not the language lovers choose?

And loving blind you have
No other light to read by
But such soft-tongued luminosities
As lovers use; and promises
Made sotto voce between moon
And moon, like ignes fatui.

Against the fire-fly seduction,
Against half-light, half-truth,
The guessed inflections
Of the tongue – Oh close your eyes
And listen inwardly lest death
Should take you by surprise.

Focus your mind, my love,
Upon the dark interstices of words,
For there truth lies uncovered,
Innocent of hands, lips, eyes,
Like a sleeping lover,
Nightly with whom death lies.

The Spindle Side

The sun is spinning strands of spider-light
Between the bobbins of a spindle tree.
Meshed in the branches' web, they shimmer. See
White Atropos! – the belladonna dame
Who stares, unmoved, the scissors in her right
Hand severing life's thread. Lachesis names
The length: she measures with a rattle-snake
The span of years, hand-spun for insect man.
And Clotho, youngest of the three, the opaque
Maid in gossamer, who spins each strand
Of ash-blonde hair from her own prophetic head.
Fate's Trinity: the shears, the rule, the thread.

Distant sisters, I descend from you
By the silken thread of the spindle side.
Tease out for me some flax. Before the bride
Can be, she has to prove her fatal skill
As spinster, weaving for herself her due
In table, bed and body linen, till
Her artful fingers twist her husband in.
I am the latest *femme fatale*. I spin
A cradle cloth – a cloth for board or bier
To lay the flesh upon.
                    The bridal sheets
Are spread. You own me now, come taste the sweets
Of fate: the shears, the rule, the thread.

Oak Bride

Let earth be my pillow, and the bridal
Sheet be spread beneath this window
Where the moon rocks in its oak cradle.
And I shall sleepwalk down
The centuries until my dream grows
Rootwise; by morning I will know
How many miles four hundred years
Of water must be drawn.

All night the prodigal moon shook florins
On my bedspread. I knew then
I was a well of wishing, and all
Of me was water to be hauled.
The pull of a tree drinking is a kiss
Where darkness marries silence: by osmosis
I entered my dream. What is
Desire but reciprocal thirst?

Down centuries of drought, like a river
I softened the bed of my oak-dark lover
Till dawn broke where the great delta
Cast its branches to the sky.
Arms wide, mouth quick with desire,
Drinking my own reflection, I
Rooted there, palms cupping
The first drops like acorns falling.

Ebb Tide

If ever known, I have forgotten now
My kinship with the moon;
Desire lures: I have forgotten how
The sirens bait their song,
Or why the little fishes rise
On lines of fate to kiss
Their bright reflections in the sky-glass.
What I was once is where the sea is.

Low tide, high noon; the cold-eyed
Spirits of thermals scale the sky
On suave spirals. Streams slide
Seaward down on twisting threads,
And all that has life, by escalade
Or abseil, traces the lines of its salt
Longing back to their source. Cradle
And tomb rock on the sea's bed.

Or so it seems; but I know a place
Where no-man builds his house:
Below the gull-haunted cliffs, below clefts
Where libidinous actinia droop like breasts,
Below all this stark, unbridled thirst
There is an emptiness where not to desire
Is a lack worse than wanting. Salt air
Swings like a door to nowhere.

I am the halfway house of the unpossessed,
I am one vast window, I am roofless;
I am vacancy meditating on stasis.
Time has cast and recast its nets
Through my mind, and it has found
Nothing but an hourglass in a sea of sand.
Once, when the slack tide stiffened to possess
Me, I rose to inherit the land.

Pont Au Change: Two Views

Under the bridge or over
We are many waters, one river;
Over the bridge or under,
Many currencies, one money.

And she: explaining in her clean
French, in a creaking room of the musée
Carnavalet, that in those days
There were two currencies: one for Paris
And another for France (which is to say
Not Paris) and these two were exchanged
Under this table on that bridge over the filthy
Seine – which one could see had not changed...

And I: grappling with rates of conversion
In broken English, picture the bridge
At Naunton, sucking this smooth
Gift of green and gold into its mouth,
And the slipping sky, to spew it back
Out the other side in rucked black
And silver – consider this a fair
Exchange, but hardly the same river.

Mirror Writing

– Eleven I like. These upright
Slender citizens that state
Their singular plurality
As I and I in unison apart.
And there's an art to lines that travel
Thus in swift and static parallel...

– But eight is better:
Double-bellied, double-headed eater
Of itself. Two bubbles kissing
Emptiness, complacent buddha,
Or a hissing letter that's forever
Closing on its sting...

So, solitary skaters on the ice
And moody adolescents in the glass,
Breath-misted, pass whole minutes –
Books of hours – doodling figures
Of infinity with casual foot or finger,
While they dream of mortal limits.

Against the World's Going

It is more than the sun's going or the gold
Declivity of wheat that draws us down
Again to where the broken field
Bears a cicatrice of fencing,
And a stream
Busy beneath its ravelled covering
Burrows like a worm.

It is something more than the want
To stay the scene's dispersing,
Straddle the stream with the scant
Ligature of thought,
Or trace the barbed stitching
With the infinite caution
Of a stranger's hand.

What is it homes me here
Like the unseen pulse of radar?
Elms along the skyline stick
Their wreckage; the air stirs
With the ceaseless swell of heat.
Nothing but brimming wheat
Remains unbroken.

Somewhere in space a pointer
Flickers and stops; I scan.
Silence; the suffocation before waking,
Till, like a dream, driftwood breaks
The surface of the corn,
A young stag rears his antlers,
Stark, against the world's going.

Silence; a drowned dusk;
This dwindling earth a pebble
Rolled and rubbed
Beneath heat, like waves,
Or hands on a grain of wheat,
A crumbling husk,
Inexorably rubbing.

Nīlak

The sky began as a blue bowl scooped
And rimmed by the eye's orbit. Lilac was there,
Still and circumscribed as in lalique,
To fill a bowl's ache.

The mind would hold things in little,
Like itself, to grasp a lifetime's
Breath, a place in emptiness.
This is no blindness,

But still the smaller part of seeing.
Worlds spill slowly outward from their centre,
The eye's bowl fills and overflows
And even air must move.

Wind blows. Blue on Persian blue, *nīlak*,
A sea where crests of lilac break
To foam; and in their leaves, the soft
Lallation of the waves.

Tyranny of the Spectrum

What shall we make
Of our days, when colour,
Or memory, lack
All integrity, beckoning
All ways to some thing
Just out of the picture?

Painting by numbers,
The mind selects
Not what the soul's
Compound eye reflects,
But only the coloured pencils
The heart allows.

A child's calendar:
What could be simpler
Or less refutable
Than the seven bright
Weathers of the week –
Or more immutable?

Let's say: It was so.
Doubt not the snow's
Whiteness, the window's
Bland transparencies
Nor the seven certainties
Of the rainbow.

Call it a grey day:
In a thousand lit rooms,
Children, furious
With the snickersnack
Of scissors, shatter rainbows,
Make snow paradisiac.

Wedding Breakfast

A table in the sunlight;
Two cups of black coffee
Against the cloth's impossible white,
And a basket piled with cherries.

How constancy dazzles with its white
Lies! The shadows dark as coffee,
Two cups of tricked light,
A new moon rising on each cherry.

Still life: you can't. Even the light
Is mortal. Death is the bride in white
Tasting first fruits of loss; the slow
Ripening of cherries, blood-bright.

Degas' Ecolière

It is not every day, on meeting
Someone new, we have the chance
To size them up as they advance
And know ourselves in their retreating.

Not one foot high, and a little
Larger than life, your body's simple
In its bronze motion; straw hat tilted
A candid angle, chin lifted (perhaps
A touch too high), your bag in hand, on hip,
Above a thigh that flexes as you step
Forward to part the air that holds you up.

And I would think you less than woman
Were it not for the fact that, open
As your free approach may be
(Breasts rounded as two firm tokens
Of maturity), still you have
Some small thing to hide. Oh Eve,
Is it an apple you hold behind your back?

As she retreats, her posture alters:
Not her step, but the eye that falters
Seeing sameness so utterly unlike.
A girl's thin shoulders, a satchel
In one hand, and in the other, crooked
Up to grasp the free end of her plait,
Nothing withheld – but a holding back.

We are authorised to trespass.
And we do. A terracotta head
That has no life behind its ears
Is not a head, until we make it so.
I did not ask to see this last
Intensely private hanging-on to
Childhood, but sought it nonetheless.

And the World in a Bowl of Porridge

The barbed hand stops punishing.
Plaited and pig-tailed, obedient as dolls, we wait,
Our scored scalps tingling
Where the comb had raked.
Porridge steams in the breakfast bowls.

Then the steady hand pouring; from jug to dish
The twisted ribbon of milk;
Round bouldered shores the white silk slips
And laps the island in.
Slowly the world revolves.

Then the skilled hand spooning;
In one long viscous drip
That measures centuries
A stalactite of golden-syrup drools
And spills away.

Once there was an island; long ago
An atoll dwindled to a scattered archipelago.
In another world, on the rim of a spoon,
The snail retracts its golden horn.

Moules à la Marinière

We scoured the secret places of the creek,
Parting blistered fronds of bladder-wrack
To find the concupiscent clusters, rocked
In their granite crêche. Jack-knives prised
The molluscs out. Slick blue-blacks bruised
Slowly dull; and the sea expunged our tracks.

Bouquet of Muscadet, bouquet garni recall
The tuck and chuckle of mussels in a bucket
Behind the door. Damp and aromatic,
Steam insinuates itself into all
The kitchen clefts, and clings in briny beads
Above the flame where mussels chirp and wheeze.

I pour on wine; it seems they beg for more,
The beaked shells yearning wide as if in song –
Yet dumb – and lewdly lolling parrot-tongues.
Cream licks the back of a spoon and drawls a slur
Of unctuous benediction for this feast.
We smooth our cassocks; bow our heads; and eat.

It rained all night as though to wash away
A brininess that tanged the atmosphere:
Dreams – of forbidden fruit, of *fruits de mer*
Wrenched from their secret beds, of tastes that lay
Like sea's after-sting on the tongue. Still lingers
A trace of guilt. I wash my salty fingers.

Winter Solstice

Mais rendre la lumière suppose d'ombre une morne moitié
PAUL VALERY

See –
Now that my back is turned – the window spill
Its sudden wealth across the white wall,
And imagine how a random winter sun
Spins like a tossed coin between the scum
And spume of cloud, how branches boil in the wind
Shaking slivered light through a rain-tricked window.

Argentum vivum, pools of watered silk
Spangling the bridge's belly, or spilt moon-milk
Curdled in the coldest heart of winter.
I looked for a way into the centre
And found only my head's shadow there,
Fraught with each stray scribble of hair,

Motionless, beside the holly spikes,
The still, dark clots of berries, black
In the moving silence, where a thin light shook.

Rumaucourt

(for my father)

Memory believes before knowing remembers
WILLIAM FAULKNER

Close-Up

An accident of memory reversed.
Red I can see; a lens tensed
To contain the spread of a whelming blur.
I adjust the view: the mass contracts and breathes.
Lub-dubbing its crimson life, a geranium heaves
Into focus, here, hot with the throb and thrum
Of a heart, pulsing beneath my thumb.

I.

Rumaucourt, 1937

His window opened onto monochrome.
Things were simpler then, in black and white,
He said: the clock's hands governed by the rhythm
Of the farm, the tocsin of the cockerel,
Soft alarm of clinking chains, and cattle
Restive in the barn. I tried to see
His point. I saw the cows were black and white,
But were they really Friesian? And had the kitchen
Clock stuck stubbornly at three,
Or did it ever chime? And had night fallen
Early there – or did the camera lie?

Josianne

After-dinner faces cloud the kitchen;
Empty glasses. Hands forever reaching
For the bottle. A small beribboned child
Muzzles her snarling brother with a sieve.
She holds her audience captive as she smiles
For the box. They say it never lies,
Arrests its image, holds the captor hostage.

Andrée

Home-maker, child-bearer, wife
And servant, mistress of grief.
Habit mocked her with 'Mother'
Though she just subsists, neither
Possessed nor quite possessing,
Set back from her brood, guessing
At their fledgling schemes to fly
The nest, or cuckoo-greedy,
Squeeze her from the hearth she warmed
With her own womb, burning, torn
From her now. She stands detached,
Not quite managing to touch
Her husband's shoulder. The gap
Is framed, fixed, in white and black.

Robert

Here is a man who shares my father's blood,
But not his name. I ponder that.
Who measured out the portions? Were they fair,
Or did this stranger get the better share?
I'd have to dig below the skin to where
The stuff shunts breathlessly its red load
Through the tunnelled flesh, to find the answer.

Not here. Not now. He lives another tense.
The chair-back takes the burden of his laughter
Silently. He's looking at his daughter;
Feels her pull and loves the way she winds him
Round her little finger. Does he sense
His wife behind him?

Sons. Les Sons. Les Sens

Guillaume, Yves, Arsène. Roll the strange
New tastes across your tongue, mouthing a child's
Vague grace before a meal: E oh me, Amen.
Spell me a face for each name. I'm reading through
You squinting one-eyed through a Glacier Mint
Sucked smooth as a camera's lens. There are two
Men amused by a muzzled boy. Recall again
My cousins, much removed: Guillaume, Yves, Arsène.

The Go-Between

Close the book and fold them into dark.
Now tell me why a one-eyed world goes flat
And how I should measure absence with a look
And how I might cover distance with my hand
And how I should trace my blood in white and black.
Close your eyes; shrink down behind my lens.
Now show me where day begins, night ends.

II.

First Light

When first we woke in that place, we may have sensed
Our own desertion there,
Lying in the high room, in the too high bed,
Searching the light as it edged on the window-sill
Too slowly, and eight flies in aimless quadrille
Troubled the tall air.

At cock-crow, memory crept back like a truant lover
Mocking our wise fear
Of the stiff furniture, the dust cover
Of sleep, till we longed to abandon what we'd become
Beneath sleep in that strange bed and abandoned room
Waiting for light to appear.

We are ourselves and more, waking to what
We've come for; finding more
Than we want or can ever push back, like the slow light
On the window-sill, the heavy sheets, the air,
The importunate tug of the blood, our being here
Waking to Rumaucourt.

The Kitchen

Soft shift of air in milky somnolence;
Stir, but do not wake.
I finger-coax the door; obedient
Somnambulist returning to its frame.
A sour lactic sweetness trails a foam
Of bubbles in its wake.

Nothing's greatly changed. The table charts
An archipelago
Of wine-stains. Coral atolls, skerries, scars
Of civilisation in the woodgrain sea.
A ghosted clockface haunts the wall at three,
Mocked by its shifting shadow.

Their faces ghost elsewhere; but someone's left
His smile in a glass
Beside the sink. The loving bubbles cling
Where white and pink a plaster rictus drifts
In mute suspense: smothered laughter doubling
His collapsed lips' loss.

When sourmouthed morning comes, he'll find them both –
The laughter and the loss –
Swallowing grief with the inward gasp of mirth,
Putting senescence in its place, teeth
In theirs, hiding pointless truth beneath
The necessary false.

Beneath the door, a strand of strawlight slipping
Dawn's drawn lot.
She'll try to sweep it out, the woman sleeping
Cruelly bare without her body's apron
Bundled here, neat, far from the undone
Flesh, its careful knot.

Thresholds

Loosed in the yard like gangaboon hens, to grub
For treasure sunk in mud;
Flouting *défense de, verboten, forbidden*, we robbed
Decay of its blistered carapace, breaking the crust
In greed for communion: crumbs in our hands and rust
In our mouths, like the taste of blood.

Swung by day from disastered beams, swung
Above splintered kingdoms of straw,
Tossed like chaff through asthmatic halflight, spun
Into darkness, drunk on parabola, high in the crooked
Rafters' cage, stalling the ripcord, hooked
On the lapse of the backward yaw.

Then hunger gnawed. Rats among the rafters
Drove us from the barn
Towards the tense meniscus of their laughter:
Trembling at the window's lucid brink,
Between their bubble and the blackness, shrink
Or burst, worlds turned.

That night we ate off plates despair had laid
Deep in the beaten earth
Against the pulsing forces as they ploughed
The Flemish trench. For years the coulter chucked
Up shards, yet some survived, wise to the shock
Of grit between our teeth.

What threshold we had crossed to reach the coils
Of curdled light that wound
Us in, we did not ask; nor why the spoiled
Supper lay stonecold in Andrée's place
Beside the fire, nor why her dumb face
Cried tears down.

Second Light

In sleep, voiceless, calling out for water
In a strange tongue,
Not mine, she came, as if to her own daughter,
Spilling silver droplets on the floor
Beside my bed, her hand, trembling where
The chill glass hung.

Darkness slid across my tongue, the taste
Of earth, cold, aching
Down my throat. A cut geranium laced
Through her nightgown's trellis, shivered towards the breeze
Where soldiers lay beneath their sodden wreaths
Of poppies, beyond waking.

It sprung at the prying tip of each knife flicked
By Arsène in the barn:
Scattering rats across the beams he'd pick
Them off like flies, till there was nothing left
To kill, and boredom on its belly crept
Away from the empty farm.

It wilted in a vase beside her bed,
Sick, the spoiled daughter
With her baby, crying like a child
For her mother, only now, to come and take
The shameful thing away. I woke,
Crying out for water.

The Window

Small rain; the slow crow drawl
Across fields to where
Distance hangs like a net curtain drawn
Against knowing. Irksome blankness, me blinking
The mote from my eye, and the fly-speck inching
The grey mesh of air.

To push this thing aside, throw wide the sky's
Window, breast the jutting
Cloud-sill and transcribe land's ancient lie,
From scattered reams of fields, tracing the cursive
Signature of contour, road, and river,
Clear beyond doubting.

Mist rolls in like a sudden sea; my name
Wades through my breath –
Glass clouds if you look too close or hard –
Each finger traces a path to the same yard,
The same six hens fretting the dumb
Palimpsest of earth.

III.

The Betrayal

Turning another page, I felt time leap
A ragged breach, the heart tricked out of a beat
That lasted twenty years. Colour spilled
Across the page like a bad mistake, spoiled
The bib and tucker ways of black and white,
And caught me there, betraying my ignorance
Like a zip undone: the dumb innocence
Of a smile as easy as a camera's parting
Gesture, gift of a Medusa, thwarting
The hand's escape, the trapped bird's flight.

Looking across my shoulder at their faces
Now, their buckled smiles and our neat cases
On the doorstep, Andrée's halfway hand
And her eternal hanky, I understand
The true and hopeless sense of *Au revoir*
As they had meant it. Their appeal with our
Unkind parole vouchsafed: *Au r'voir – au r'voir.*
Still, *she* kept her word, for in the utter
Silence of this frame, her fingers flutter
Still: *l'adieu suprême des mouchoirs.*

The Return

A child's geography. If nothing moved
Or altered, I might sense the dark way back
Through corridors of poplars where the louvred
Air breathes balsam; past the girl in black
Beside the cemetery, two chickens dangling
By the legs from either hand; the rabid
Dog after its tail; the voices wrangling
Over cattle prices, and the dazed
Beasts waiting; past the yellow mitten
Waving from the fence – *tout droit!* until

34

The gate, the yard, the window where I'd written
Names, all welcomed my return.
                             And still
I'm on the outside looking in. *Ouvre-moi*
Ta porte pour que je puisse te revoir.

* * *

Douai, Cambrai, Écourt, Rumaucourt.
It is not names that change or disappear,
But faces and their features, like a rumour
Tongues and time pull out of shape. Here
I can turn my back on the unanswered door,
Knowing who stands behind, my hand light
On the latch to lift and open, ready to show
Me round, knowing my way in, as out,
By heart, a journey of the blood, the slow
Footfall of diastole and systole through the night.

* * *

Turning back, I leave things as I found them:
Place in its pot the bright geranium,
By the door in a yard at the heart of Rumaucourt,
Between Douai, Cambrai, the Pas de Calais and the Nord,
In the crease of a map scuffed blank by endless folding.

Only the map of the blood I'll keep, to tuck
In here, and here; the spacious holdings
Of the head; the heart's soft ruck.

Riddle

I am the difficult silk that slides from your grasp,
I am lace petticoats and the knee-high swirl,
I am an old sea-captain's white moustache,
I am the perm that will not hold its curl,
I am the land's dropped slip and rising shift,
I am a piece of froth, a bagatelle,
I am relinquishment and eternal theft,
I am a gesture of greeting and farewell.

Lost Property

Kneel, and let us pray for the departed:
A sulphurous incense chokes the station vaults,
A pigeon coughs; the platform is deserted.
Guilty-eyed, while others slept in prayer
I scoured the hassock's cross-stitch for some fault
As though it were my soul; and found none there.

A labour of devotion: pious kisses
Smothering the cushion where my knees
Grew numb and bore the imprint of those stitches.
Burden of the Cross. A priest intones,
Feet shuffle for Communion to ease
The weight, and catch the last train home.

The rails are silent, empty as the aisle
When rush-hour's past. A platform sweeper brushes
Up confetti into piles.
It's growing dark. A thin girl stands and watches
As he sweeps the crumbs that drowsy birds
Have missed. I wake. And there are words
For this; but none so fittingly expressed
As by my own hand cupped around my breast.

Conjurings

If ever I was your wish –
And only if –
Then take me now for granted.

But mundane magicks only work and last
When conjurer and conjured, rules and craft
Have learnt by mutual heart;
And through this pact
Rehearse, perform, perfect their double act.

If, with our simple art
You should grow disenchanted,
And I, bereft of sometime magic,
Seem nothing more
Than white, domestic rabbit –

Then, and only Then,
Remember this
If ever I was your wish.

Spinster

This day beggars description,
Though smoke hangs in autumn
Stagnancies above the churchyard
And the sky wears its yeast of cloud

Like the bloom on a damson.
I had thought my book of the seasons
Too big for summer thus to shrink
To the foolish dimensions of an ice-rink

In June. Well, I was wrong.
The year has put its clothes on
Inside out. We wake to new confusions
Of frost and the wrung

Sweetnesses of Summer, finding
Only the sourness of apples, blackberries
Hard as nipples, no windfalls
But the petals of a stunned rose.

What do I have to show for this
August body, but the stasis
Between youth and prime, hiatus
Of flesh and fruiting, a caught

Breath? The speckled spider builds its net
From inside out, then outside in,
Brute purpose mazily zigzagging;
It homes to the centre and waits.

I rock on my heels and test
My breath's spillage on the air.
I shall fold it with the weather
For safe keeping, in a camphor chest.

Tonight I undress more carefully
Than usual, shedding skin after skin
Like silk underthings, till I
Am nothing but a blond skein

Of beginnings. Tomorrow, or
The day after, or the day after
That, from the outside in,
I shall consider the art of spinning.

In Absentia

It is like this:
The slipper wants a foot. At dawn
The mind has fingers,
Shapes itself to things.
From air it moulds the gaunt El Greco toes,
The vaulting instep; and the heel
It holds a moment, like an egg, to feel
The cool weight in its palm.
It puts the slipper on.

And then it is like this:
Lop-sided, one-slippered, odd,
The mind limps off to find the other
Shoe, the shoe, the other foot.
See what the mind has done, has left undone –
Ah, calves knees thighs, and the night comes.
It is no good; I get no further
Than the ground on which you stood.
The slipper wants a foot.

Epithalamium

Ask not, this night, how we shall love
When we are three-year lovers;
How clothes, as lapsing tides, as love,
May slide, three summers over;
Nor ask when the eye's quick darknesses
Throw shadows on our skin
How we shall know our nakedness
In the difference of things.

Ask not whose salty hand turns back
The sea's sheet on the shore,
Or how the spilt and broken moon rides
Still each wave's humped back –
Ask not, for it is given as my pledge
That night shall be our sole inquisitor,
Day our respondent, and each parting as the bride
And groom, an hour before their marriage.

The Cowled Traveller

Connoisseur of the medlar,
Of soft ripenesses and the hard –
Fruit hawker, egg pedlar.

Devotee of the straight
And narrow, low-lier, upright
Always in your ways.

Caster of seeds, dove breeder –
St Francis of Assisi
Setting the caged birds free

To burst upwards like salt
Spray pluming between rocks,
Or the flung sparks of Cyclops.

My one-eyed night-watchman
Sou'westered, O my Capuchin –
What schemes are you hatching?

Song

Others have been laid out like this before us –
Side by sleeping side, softness to my softness,
Bone to your bone – and have dreamed that neither grass
Nor stone can grow where flesh, frame merge thus.

Below an hourglass sky, the lovers stretch,
Endless flotsam cast beyond the world's reach,
Together lie, heedless of the sun's touch,
Or grit of time whose slow sift mounts beneath.

Others have been laid out like this before us –
Side by sleeping side, ashes to her ashes,
Dust to his dust – who dream still as the tireless
Rain washes their stones; between, the simple grass.

The Benediction

What was it stooped to bless
This day's unloveliness
Amid the surburbia of crocus
And gaudy polyanthus,
When, behind the window's glass
The sudden girl in turquoise
Stooped laughingly to kiss –
As if for my emptiness –
His unseen, upturned face?

Mother, Baby, Lover
(for Vanessa)

When in the darkness
Behind closed lids I perceive
The blind, furled fist
And the questing
Mouth, hungry as a kiss
For the place
Where she alone exists –

I think with infinite compassion
Of all the breast-
Starved lovers of our world undressing
You to drink at this
Soft inverted cup of maternal bliss
In gratitude, and less
Than ignorance of what they miss.

Night Passage

Between the differing colour of our skins
There is more than the stars' confusion
Or conspiracies of night. At your birth
The gibbous moon turned by your mother's
Side, finding such fullness in
Your blond transparencies that even
The tides rose up against their ebbing.

Under a swarthy pelt I rocked
All night, waiting for dawn to break.
I could not sleep for the marvel
Of ivory stretched at my brackish
Side. Watching the cold stars shiver
In my wake, I have known more than dark
– O my white, insentient freight.

When dawn came, I neither slept
Nor woke. It seemed that sunlight crept
Like cinquefoil up the blue-veined trellis
Of your hand; knowing the moon had laced you
Where you lay, and you would wake
Like Gulliver, to a strange land
And a stranger's sun-dark hand.

Villanelle

Can you be jealous of the sun
Who's blind, and has no hands to bless
The nut-brown body of my sin?

The rain has fingers, and it shuns
No crevice: when you consider this
Can you be jealous of the sun?

I am as modest as the season's
Temperatures when I undress
The nut-brown body of my sin,

Loving no one but the long stain
Of my shadow in the grass.
Can you be jealous of the sun?

It's only thirst for bone and skin
That makes the avid heat caress
The nut-brown body of my sin.

Self-love consumes. When you have seen
The burnished husk of emptiness –
Can you be jealous of the sun,
The nut-brown body of my sin?

The Womanhood

It was the colour of incense
And it drove men wild.
She wore it like the wind
And the devil smiled
To see such innocence
In a grown-up child.

Subtleties she practised
Till they had her by heart –
Played her like the psaltery
So no man could part
Her fingers' lattice
From their naked art.

It was the flame's syllable
And the ferryman's fee.
She sung men to heaven
Where she turned them free
With the taste of obol
Where her name should be.

Hand Upon Hand
(after Harley Lyric no.1)

Hand stole from hand   unlawful handful
Hand other handfuls   with full hand fouls
Hand fondles hand   in lustful hand-thrall
Though hand for free hand   would unhand all.

Pseudo-Narcissus

I said: the reflection of Narcissus
Was a woman.
What are you, then, but the crisis
Of my own surfacing – a face,
These eyes, this mouth, breaking
Myriad and marvellous
To drink the poisonous
Vacancy of air.
And I am drowning.

This is the poem reversed –
The diver in the backward-running
Film springing feet-first, perverse
From an impossible medium.
Somewhere I took a wrong turning.
You? Victim? –
Shatter the sweet reflection.
I am seduced utterly
By my own seduction.

Double

Darling – I am not what I appear:
Single-hearted with my long brown hair
Plaited for safe-keeping.

Something I have undone –
A stray wisp, a random
Provocation – say, a grass clipping –

Has set my brown mane wild,
Casting oats in our careful field
While both our hands were sleeping.

This is no dream. Double I see
And am, courting duplicity
Like the suave surface of a stream

Flowing in two directions.
Am I the warped reflection,
The undertow, or the still scene

That witnesses its distortion,
Loving no less the portions
Of its selfhood that remain?

I am none and all.
The body in its close thrall,
The deceiving eye and mind.

I am my mother's daughter.
Cover my face with my hands,
My hands with water.

Dead-Heading

A rose, crimson,
Undoing itself in my hand
Whorl by petalled whorl,
Velvet and internal:
A flagrant secret planned
To unfurl itself and spill
Petal by whorled petal
Its rash contraband.

Too ripe, too late, the hour
Opens on us like a wound
This pulse of love, its flower.

Foxglove

Who taught the cunning little vixen
Manicure? – Sure, she's fixing
To make a kill, a half moon waxing

Nacreous on each fingernail.
Two bees jostle the same bell,
Fumbling the purple fingerstall.

Nonchalant, she slips a glove
On either slender paw, as if
Murder were mere elegance of love.

Wheat into Darnel

In the seed of Wheat there lieth obscurely the seminality of Darnel, although in a secondary or inferiour way, and at some distance of production; which nevertheless if it meet with convenient promotion, or a conflux and conspiration of causes more powerful then the other; it then beginneth to edifie in chief, and contemning the superintendent form, produceth the signatures of its self.

SIR THOMAS BROWNE, Pseudodoxia Epidemica

For Darnel: see Walloon.
Come now, see a black-haired
Green-eyed Pole in a Frenchman's
Skin. See Lolium Tementulum –
See Virgil's drunken tare.

Your colleague, your accomplice,
I am your comrade – not in arms –
But wishing so: to splice
And graft our loves, illicit
Husbandry, your palm to my palm.

See how I till our tongue
For grains of you, sifting the dry
Lexicon of husk, ear, awn
Till I am cognate with that corn
Wherein your seed lieth obscurely.

Nothing will ever grow
Without impurities of Nature.
So come: eyes to the rich furrow,
Your hand upon mine, sowing
Our self's own signature.

Eve Sharing

That time, the apple went clean in half
At the first fine stroke of the knife
That severs lovers, leaving the flesh ungrazed,
The divided heart. So, Eve, as Libra poised,
Stood weighing the equal halves, amazed
At her own fairness; her child eyes
Measuring the clean flesh, circumference
Of sin, the love of sharing – even
Down to the pip in its ebony chalice
Whose kernel is milk-white, miraculous
As a child's milk tooth, shed once
And never to be had again.

'It is the warp of me'

It is the warp of me,
A flaw ingrained, or love-knot
Whorling to its heart
What should be separate
To keep a soul upright.

A slight obliquity
Of mind, perhaps, that grows
With use: unseasoned house!
No door will close
But through and through love blows.

Suspended Verdict

If cardiologists lack skill
To stitch a broken heart
Or say what part
Of love is diastole,

Or why, a full minute,
The wrong-way blood drove hard
Against the heart
And all that's in it –

Then who am I to tell
What caused this thing to break
Its metre, making
Simple heaven, pure hell?

Siren Song

This is the season of shipwreck;
Although you would not know it
From the calm beatitude of night,
And stars so singly constant in their track.

This is the season of shipwreck
When every bone bespeaks a portion
Of the skeleton it will become,
And the mortal marrow aches.

This is the season of shipwreck
That mouths to you with ragged winter lips:
A keening of the sea, where lapsed
Souls hug themselves and rock.

Listen. The sound the waves make –
A sound of aftermath, as when the siren,
Softly in her sleep, sings that serene
Shore, where only hearts can break.

Meteorology

Damn these predictable forecasts –
The tautology of life and art,
Let's have a new theme:
The grass is brown, the sky is green.

All summer I sunned myself and sinned.
I didn't burn, but I turned brown
Enough to burn the face of man.
Oh, Hell reserved its flames for autumn
And it's winter now; well, we have ash
For weather...

        Come, let us wash
The smirched horizon, bury the good
Ash, and before this small god,
This notional ember, kneel together.
Breathe on the coal, my love, for this
Is our hearth, our single heart, faith's
Orison, and one true weather.

Chorus Line

Somewhere in amongst the lace
And hairpins, mothballs, liquorice
And once bitten twice shy sticky sugar mice
It's a question of finding one's voice.

Listen – even if you can't hear this –
I'm not the first, and certainly the least
Singular of persons to admit a crisis.
The muse, not I, has laryngitis.

Silence? We'll call it a tacit truce.
Besides, there's six of us
And we can't all speak at once,
Even if we had all found our voices.

Better to hold our peace...
But listen: we sing with our eyes,
And flabby breasts and bellies –
No less, or it's all lies.

The tea-lady brings me solace
And no prose. Beneath her bodice –
Crisp as a trellis of ice –
Flames the impossible rose.

Beggar-Poets

Speechless, artless, toothless,
Who mouth a living round this
Crust of life, softening
The jagged edges with our tongue;

Till it becomes as smooth,
As pliant, as a half-baked truth;
Small-talk, lip-service –
The soft evasive answer of a kiss.

Sightless, songless, mindless,
We are the breadwinners passing
Endlessly between (give us
This day) the profit and the loss.

Have nothing, nothing want
Beneath the bounty of a gaunt
Sky; listening to the wind
Hollow my cupped hand.

Song Without Words

(after Vermeer's 'Woman Tuning a Lute')

How can we hear with our eyes?
As if by listening we might
See chromatic shadow, or light
Plucked from a string of pearls.

We have been brought here, not
To learn harmony, but
Double counterpoint, mute
Music of the play of light;

And we are left with our senses orphaned,
Knowing only we must see before
Looking, feel before touching, hear
Before listening. We are old to learn.

There is a woman, a window,
A map and a lute. There is
Concentration and repose;
Light improvising on shadow.

And on this slack, invisible string
She works, the belly of the lute
Against her belly, and the light
Across her forehead tautening.

Blind to the shifting tracts
Of Europe, dim against the wall,
Her element is intensely local.
A face turned, listening, rapt,

To the window's emptiness. Tuning,
We have become the peg of her lute,
Instruments of his palette,
Light from a plucked string.

Ter Borch to His Students

This is not a matchbox trick:
I'm asking you to balance three
Spheres on the ridge of a pyramid –
Two on the slope and one at the apex.
Consider this your matrix.

Your spheres will be arranged
In descending order of scale:
From a woman's head, say,
To the dimensions of an apple.
Trust now, and they won't fall.

They won't fall once you have
The acute and the oblique angle
In tune, and the geometries of love
Begin to take a form, as hands
Will take the roundness of an apple.

For love's an art that discloses
A design – a formal correspondence –
Even in the most artless of poses;
Takes as its theme a woman delousing
A child, and makes of it an instance

Of such harmony as music makes
Among spheres. Paint so that
Your art transcends all logic –
So that your heart defies
Even the gravity of disbelief:

Though pyramids return to sand
And worlds from their orbits topple,
Still holds this ratio of faith, blind
As the stars in their ecliptic, simple
As a child's hands round an apple.

Chant de la rue des Rosiers

I am learning
Slowly this street's
Language, being
Not just foreign,
But inchoate –
A blind mute:

Something, without
Tense or gender,
Loveless as a mouth
Pressed on glass,
Pitching its voice
Against loss.

How would you transcribe
The minor mode
Of an only child
Singing so, so softly
Without words
To itself? –

Or the dogged cry
Of a beggarwoman –
Oyé umpyé
Oyé umpyé –
Innured to its own
Bleak threnody. –

Or the wail
Of the synagogue door
(My clock-on-the-wall,
My calendar)
And the sudden chants
Torn from silence.

It is Saturday.
The bell tips to its clapper.
Not only the Jews
Are hungry.
Some sing, some cry
For their supper.

Some dance;
Have you heard
Of the stripteaseuse
Across the road?
She moves in silence
But the meaning's clear.

It is quite still,
But for the swivelling wind
On the window sill,
Saying: Sing, sing,
My squeaky hinge.
And I will.

Impostor

Don't think that I don't know your games,
You understudy muse, with your acrostic
Heart and chiffon soul – slick
Gloss on bloodless lips.

I do. I know the closet where
You lock your anagramatising mind,
Word-flowers, word-animals
With pop-in legs and petals.

How, in the dark you take them out,
Your poets, one by one, and count
Them; tucking each bauble back
Bright-brittle, in Christmas wrapping.

And Oh when you hang them on your tree,
Save on some branch a place for me –
Sweet victim – your cutest fairy:
And I shall honour you with such

Howls as would haul black hags
And matted beasts from their lairs,
Dragging the reins of your blonde hair,
Bare on the bare back of nightmare.

That's how we play. No six to start,
No lies, no honesty. Only the heart
With its four black holes – See?
There *are* no rules. Now hand me that key.

History Goes to Work

The soft-boiled egg is emptied
But makes a humpty-dumpty head
Reversed. Numbskull! Bald pate!
You know the spoon's importunate
Knock knock will wake the dead.

The silver spoon lies on its back
And spoons the room all up-
Side-down but never spills a drop:
The ovoid walls adapt their laws
And never show a crack.

The egg lies in the silver spoon
And yolkless words lie on the tongue
And all that's in the spoon-shaped room
Swears it is square; no books
Were cooked. The egg is done.

Remorse rests in its velvet drawer
Lapped in the sleep of metaphor,
The soul rests in the open palm
And will not put its shell back on,
And calmly waits for more.